Dedicated to my son Jack, and my loud, scruffy, little dog, Benji

The dog called Scruff, who lost his woof!

Written and illustrated by Eve Williams

There was a boy called Jack, he had a dog called Scruff...

...And my goodness, did he like to woof?!

He would bark at other dogs,

… or if he saw cat!

He would bark at the shed, if he thought he'd heard a rat!

He would bark at other animals
that popped up on TV...

...Or at anyone walking past the house he could see!

He was a ball of energy, he was very proud,

for a dog so small, he was very loud!

But one day Scruff woke up and his *'woof'* had disappeared!

He tried to bark, *"it's gone!"*, he feared!

For days and days, Scruff was as quiet as a mouse,

his family quite enjoyed the peace and quiet around the house...

But one day, Jack saw how
Scruff looked so sad…

He thought.. 'How can I get
back the *woofy* dog I once had?'

So, he pretended to be a cat,

He bought a fake rat!

He came to the door,
wearing a postman's hat!

He invited over his friend with his pet husky,

and they browsed through animal shows on TV!

He called the vets to see what they thought...

But they didn't know, so that call was cut short...

Then he browsed the web,
for hours a day,

but he decided, he'd just have to
find his own way...

He made a list, then made a start...

...At all the things he knew, that should get Scruff to bark!

He took him for a walk, where
other dogs would be,

but Scruff just walked past
them so quietly...

He fell to the floor, and
pretended to cry...

But Scruff just sniffed him,
and walked on by...

No matter what Jack tried,
there was just no sound!

Scruff just sat silent, looking
sad, with a frown.

Jack felt sorry for Scruff, with each day that passed by...

But then, he thought of one more thing he could try!

So that night, Jack made a wish after dark,

he wished that tomorrow, Scruff would just *bark*!

When Jack woke up with
the morning's light,

he threw Scruff's ball and
screamed with delight!

For the sounds that he heard were...

WOOF WOOF
WOOF WOOF!

They were both so pleased,
Scruff was back to being Scruff!

About the author

Hello, young readers! I'm Eve Williams. I'm a busy mom, juggling work and studying, but I've always loved art and writing poetry ever since I was little. After having my own son, I discovered the joy of sharing children's books with him, which sparked my desire to create my own. This book about a boy and his dog is just the beginning—I hope to make more (when I can find the time). I hope your little one enjoys this story!

Printed in Great Britain
by Amazon